SERVICE STATION
COLLECTIBLES

SERVICE STATION
COLLECTIBLES

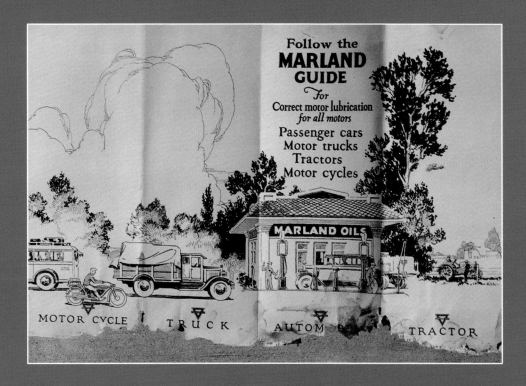

Follow the
MARLAND GUIDE
For
Correct motor lubrication
for all motors
Passenger cars
Motor trucks
Tractors
Motor cycles

MARLAND OILS

MOTOR CYCLE   TRUCK   AUTOMOBILE   TRACTOR

RICK PEASE

Schiffer Publishing Ltd

77 Lower Valley Road, Atglen, PA 19310

Dedication

This book is dedicated to everyone who has encouraged me along the way...my family, my friends and collectors, and vendors that provided the memorobilia.

I cannot go without mentioning my brother Mike Pease, my daughters Nikki Whitley and Debra Shaffer...AND a very special junker-to-be, my new grandson, Daniel Shaffer.

Library of Congress Cataloging-in-Publication Data

Pease, Rick.
Service station collectibles / Rick Pease.
p. cm.
ISBN 0-88740-934-2 (paper)
1. Service stations--Collectibles--United States--Catalogs.
2. Petroleum industry and trade--Collectibles--United States--Catalogs.
I. Title.
NK808.P43 1996
629.28'6'0973075--dc20
95-42727
CIP

ISBN: 0-88740-934-2
Printed in Hong Kong

Published by Schiffer Publishing Ltd.
77 Lower Valley Road
Atglen, PA 19310
Please write for a free catalog.
This book may be purchased from the publisher.
Please include $2.95 for shipping.
Try your bookstore first.

Contents

	Introduction	7
Chapter One	Gasoline Pumps	8
Chapter Two	Maps	33
Chapter Three	Motorcans	51
Chapter Four	Pin-backs, Name Badges, Signs, Globes	58
Chapter Five	Signs	91
Chapter Six	Pictorial Cans	130
Chapter Seven	Soda Signs	153

Acknowledgments

A very special 'Thanks' to my friend Terry St. Clair and his family for their contribution to this book.

I would also like to thank the friends who allowed me to take pictures of their collectibles. Many thanks to Kyle Moore, Howard Clayburn, Charles Middleton, Kim and Mary Kokles, Scott Benjamin, Mike Worley, Barry Baker, David Anderson, David Wallace, Brad Lago, George and Melba Rook, Norm Rubenstein, Mike O'Hern, Charles Shaver, Wayne Story, Vic and Sara Raupe, Leo Mathis, Kenney Boone, Richard Eaves, and Nick Ciovica.

Introduction

I hope you will find this book, with its variety of items, to be enlightening. All attempts were made to try to provide a good sampling of items, from the small 'give-a-ways' to colorful cans, globes, and signs. The pricing method has been changed in order to benefit all—the prices stated here represent a starting point to assist you when pricing, but you will need to determine the condition and rarity of the item.

Read, Look, and Enjoy.

Chapter One

Gasoline Pumps

The following pictures are of advertising
pieces presented by the American Oil Pump
and Tank Company.

Several visible and non-visible pumps

Adjustable discharge pump

Five-gallon curb pump

'Presto Servus' meter system

Metering Singles-Doubles, Hand-Air-pump

The following pictures are of 1929 advertising pieces presented by the Bennett Pumps Corporation.

Electric Clock-Face pump

The following picture is an advertising piece from the Birmingham Machine and Foundry Company.

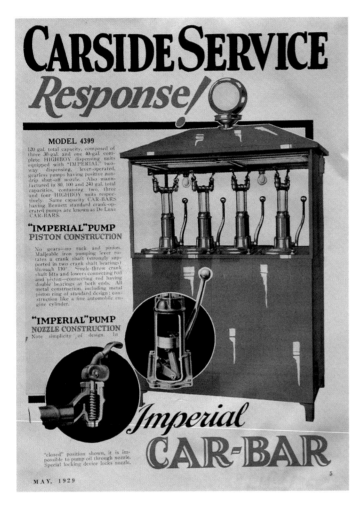

Carside service for a unique oil-dispensing unit

Five-gallon visible

The following picture is an advertising piece from the Brown Sheet Iron & Steel Co.

Filling Station and Curb Pump

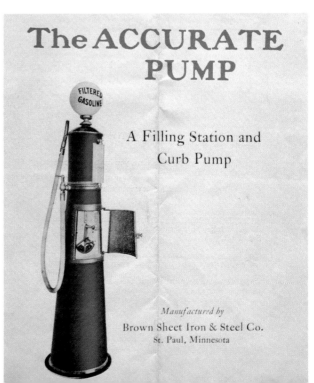

The following pictures are advertising pieces from the S.F. Bowser & Company, Inc.

Save Money with Bowser Equipment

Displays a way of dispensing both oil and alcohol from a single pump

Practice what you Preach...faster service...low in price

1921 advertising piece of Piston-Type measuring pump

Quick Turnovers with Chief-Sentury Pistor Type measuring pump

Square Sentry pump

ReelWay pump...the last word in neatness, simplicity and efficiency

Pump light for a Bowser computerized pump

The following picture is an advertising piece from the Butler Manufacturing Company:

Butler Visible Pump.

The following picture is a 1926 advertising piece from the Correct Measure Pumps Company:

The following pictures are advertising pieces from the Erie Meter Systems, Inc.:

Four Correct Measure Pumps

Erie "Triple-Check"
Visible Pump

1927 advertising piece,
clock-face electric pump

The following pictures are advertising pieces
from the Fleckenstein Visible Gasometer Co:

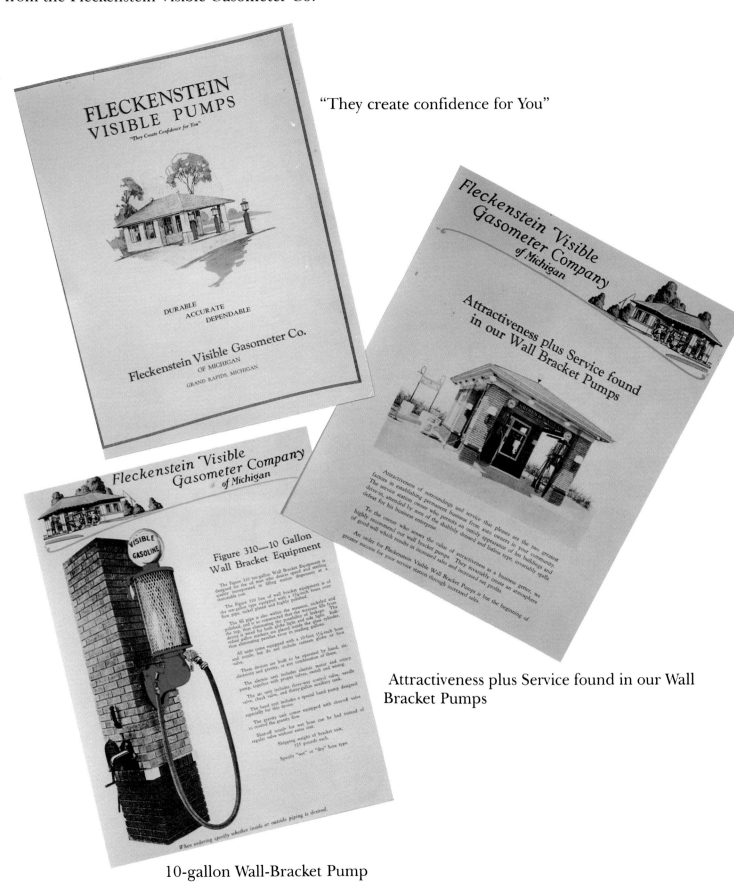

"They create confidence for You"

Attractiveness plus Service found in our Wall
Bracket Pumps

10-gallon Wall-Bracket Pump

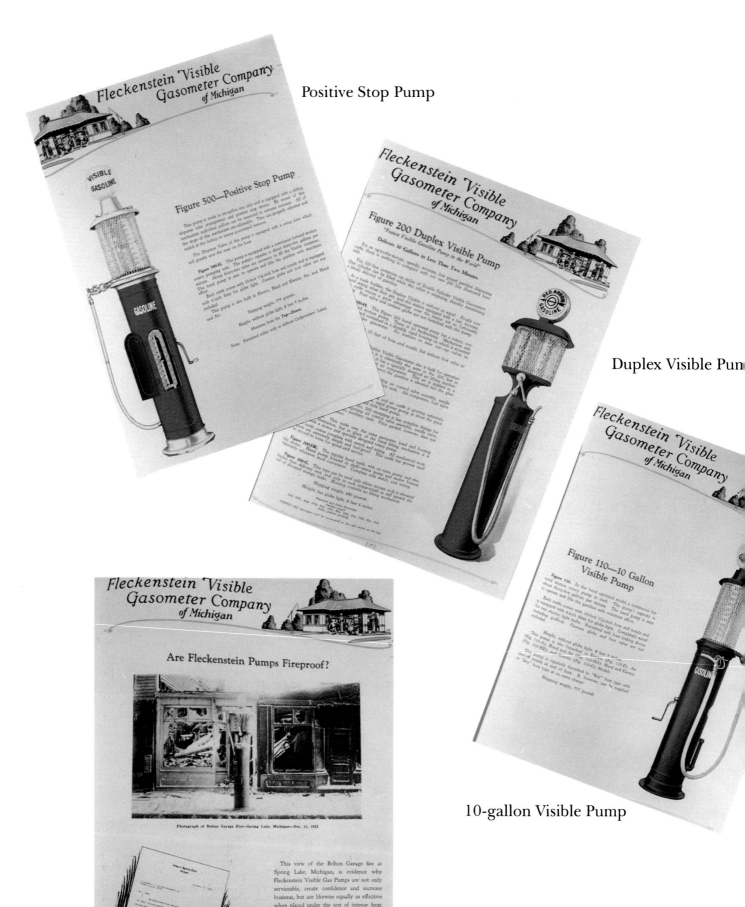

Positive Stop Pump

Duplex Visible Pump

10-gallon Visible Pump

Photo of garage fire, 1922. "Are Fleckenstein Pumps Fireproof?"

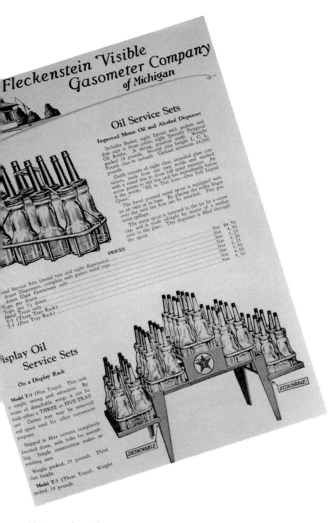

Oil Service Sets

The following picture is an advertising piece from The Groetken Pump Company:

Visible-Type Measuring System

The following pictures are advertising pieces from the Guarantee Liquid Measure Company:

Fry SuperTwin Pump

5-gallon Fry Pump

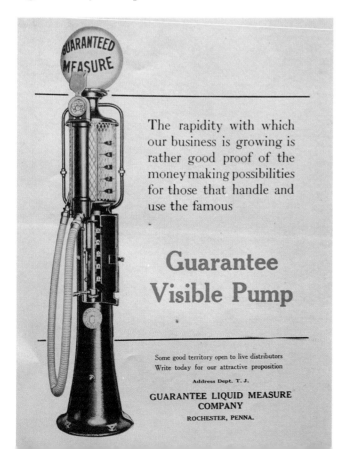

The following pictures are advertising pieces from the Gilbert and Barker Manufacturing Company:

T-94, dispenses two grades of oil

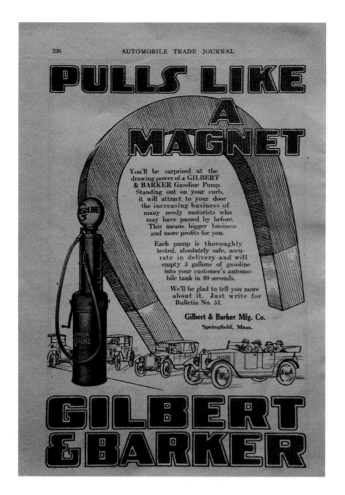

The Gilbert & Barker pump "Pulls Like a Magnet"

T-177, 10-gallon Visible Pump

T-66, Hand or Air-operated gasoline pump

T-93, Clock-face Tru-Meter & "TM" Tru-Meter

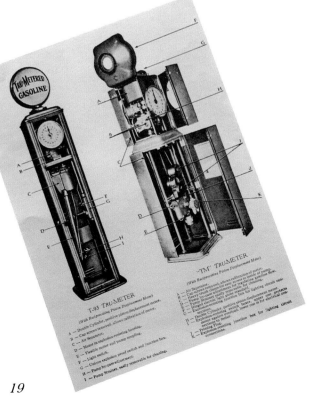

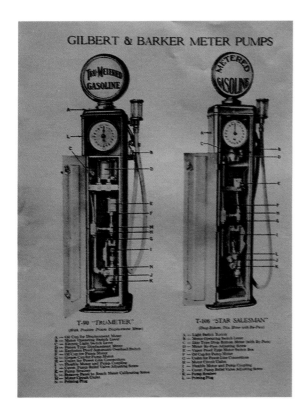

T-90, "Tru-Meter & T-106 "Star Salesman"

The following picture is an advertising piece from the Hayes Visible Pumps:

10-gallon Visible Pump

The following picture is an advertising piece from the National Recording Pump Company:

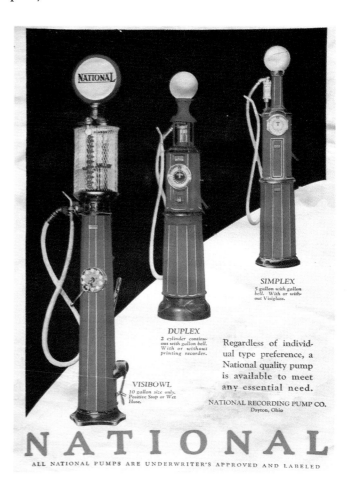

Three very collectible versions of the National Pumps

The following picture is an advertising piece from the Pneumatic Gasoline Service Company:

Electric Clock-Face Pump

The following picture is an advertising from the Shotwell Pump & Tank Company:

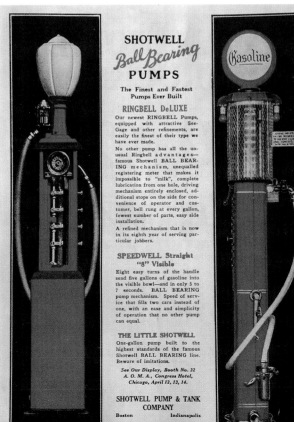

The following pictures are advertising pieces from "Rapidayton"
The Dayton Pump & Mfg. Company:

1919, Cut No. 25 Rapidayton Curb-side Pump

On the Left: Ringbell DeLuxe
On the Right: Shotwell Straight "8" Visible

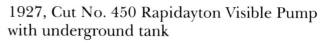

1927, Cut No. 450 Rapidayton Visible Pump with underground tank

The following pictures are advertising pieces from the Sharpsville Boiler Works Company:

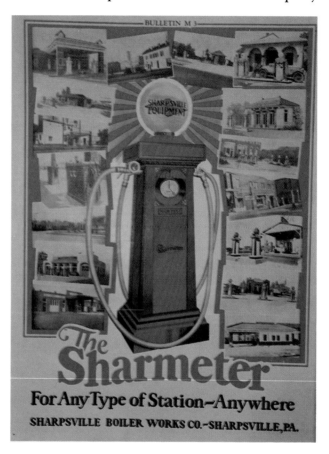

Bulletin, "The Sharmeter"

1927, Cut No. 450 Rapidayton 10-gallon Visible Pump
"The Bellboy" 5-gallon Pump
Cut No. 400 Rapidayton 10-gallon Visible Pump

M-612, Ornamental Paneled Cabinets

M-622, Double Clock-Face Pump

M-711, Plain Cabinet

ME-513, Electric Clock-Face Pump

23

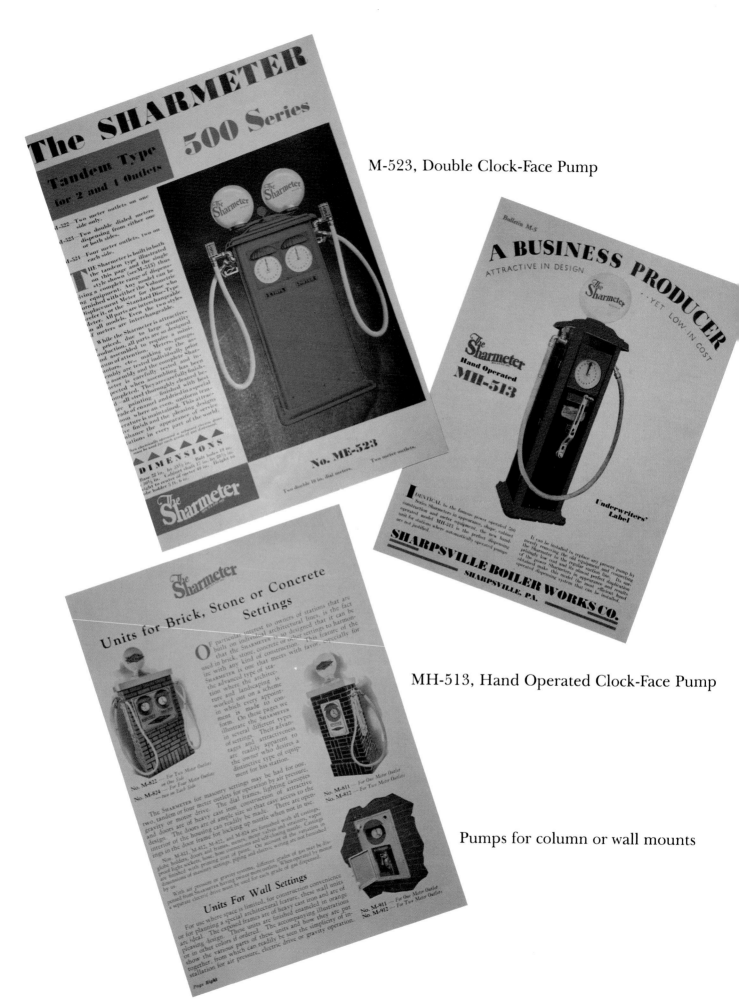

M-523, Double Clock-Face Pump

MH-513, Hand Operated Clock-Face Pump

Pumps for column or wall mounts

1927 announcement for new product

Sharfont Oil Dispenser

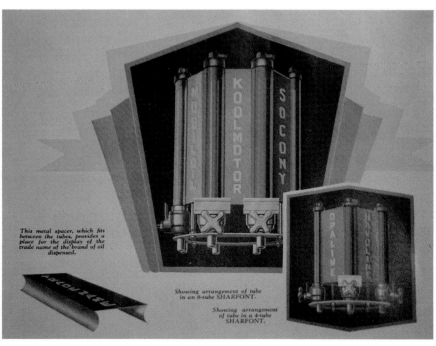

Close-up shot of the Sharfont lube dispenser

The following pictures are advertising pieces from the Southwest Pump Company:

OK-7D, 10-gallon Visible Pump

612-CSP, Computerized, Showcase Pump

Cut No. 612, Computerized, Electric Pump

The following pictures are advertising pieces from the Tokheim Oil Tank & Pump Company:

Cut 600, Visible Pumps

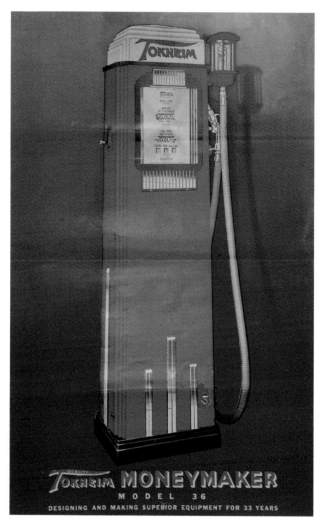

Model 36, Moneymaker Pump

Computerized, Electric Showcase Pump

Model 36, 'Twin Unit' Moneymaker Pump

The following pictures are advertising pieces from the Wayne Oil & Tank Pump Company:

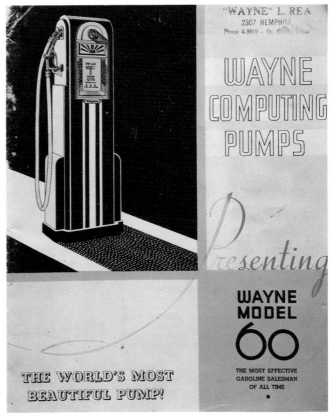

Wayne Model 60

Cut No. 276, 5-gallon Curb-side Pump

5-gallon Curb-side Pump

Wayne Model 60

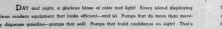

Wayne Model 50 & 60...glorious blaze of color and light

Wayne Model 50, Display Meter

Wayne Model 40

Wayne Model 861, Clock-face Pump

The following pictures are advertising pieces for Air-Scales Tire Inflating Pumps and Air Meters: (Multiple companies)

Wayne Model 40, Computing Pump

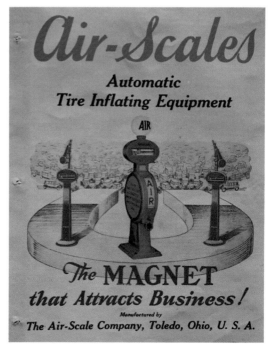

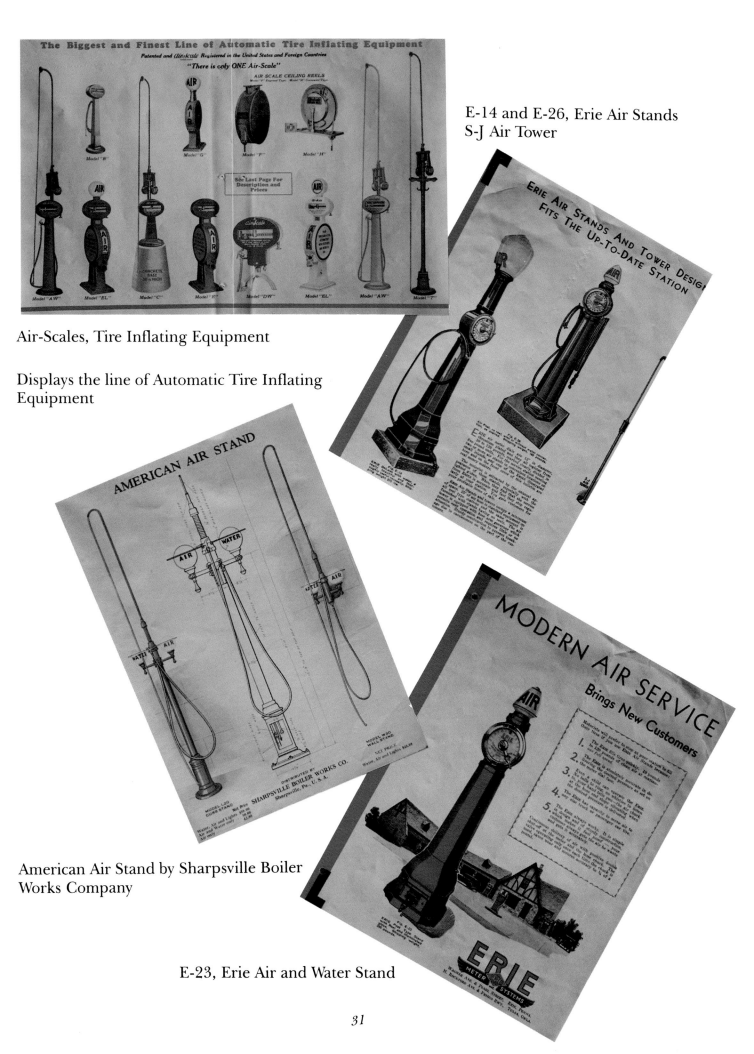

Air-Scales, Tire Inflating Equipment

Displays the line of Automatic Tire Inflating
Equipment

E-14 and E-26, Erie Air Stands
S-J Air Tower

American Air Stand by Sharpsville Boiler
Works Company

E-23, Erie Air and Water Stand

1915, Lipman Old Colonial Free Air Stations   Portable and Stationary Garage Pumps

Air & Water Meter by Service Station Equipment Company

Chapter Two

Maps

Maps are becoming more and more popular
with gasoline and oil collectors.

Richfield Motor Routes, New England and
New York, $25.

Richfield Motor Routes, New England and
New York.

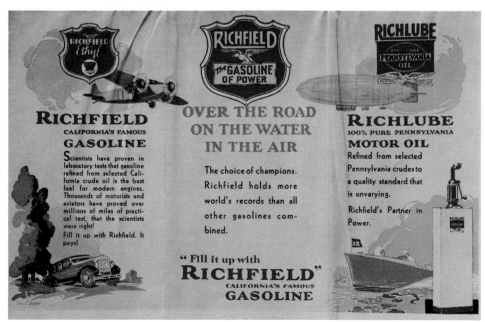

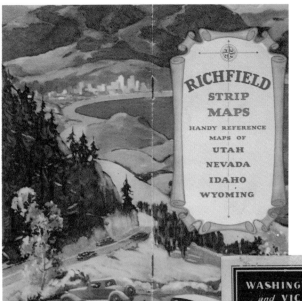

Richfield Strip Maps, Utah, Nevada, Idaho, Wyoming, $30.

Standard Pictorial Road Map of Washington, D. C. and Vicinity, $10.

Automobile Roads in Iowa, Shaffer Oil and Refining Company, $25.

Tydol flying "A", Massachusetts, Connecticut, Rhode Island, $15.

Clason's Touring Atlas of the United States and Canada, advertising Power-lube Motor Oil, $20.

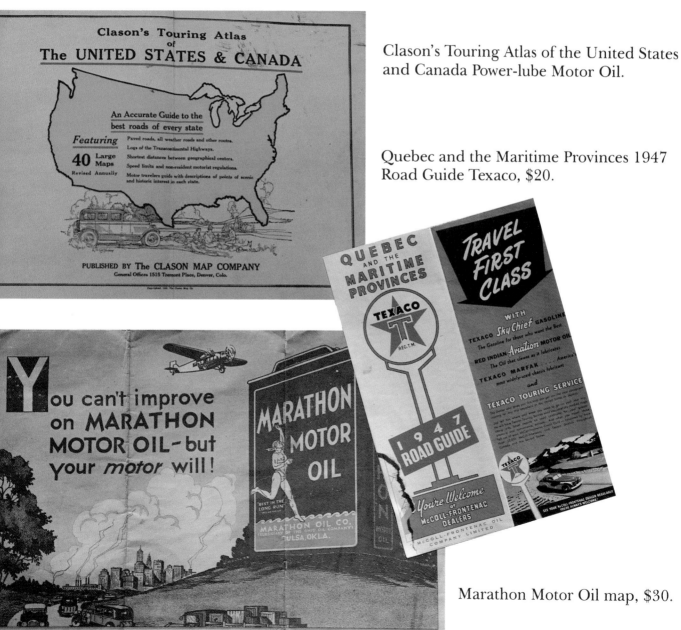

Clason's Touring Atlas of the United States and Canada Power-lube Motor Oil.

Quebec and the Maritime Provinces 1947 Road Guide Texaco, $20.

Marathon Motor Oil map, $30.

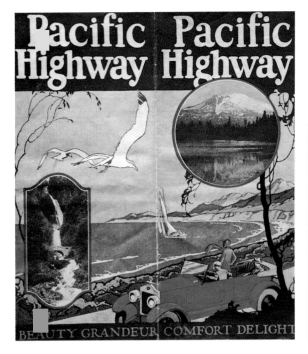

Pacific Highway, Beauty Grandeur Comfort
Delight, $15.

Richfield Strip
Maps, $20.

South Dakota Motor Trails are Calling, Red
Crown Gasoline, Standard Oil Company, $20.

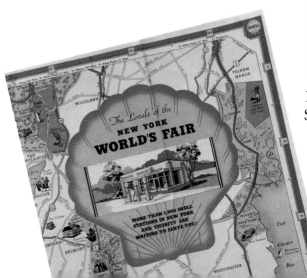

1929 Road Map, New England, Allstate Tires,
$15.

New York World's Fair, Shell Oil Company,
$25.

1932 Road Map, Pennsylvania Shell Oil Company, $20.

Metropolitan Map, Chicago, Shell Oil Company, $20.

1931 Road Map, Maine, Shell Oil Company, $25.

1930 Road May, Southern New England, Shell Eastern Petroleum Products, Inc., $20.

1929 Shell Road Map, Minnesota, Shell Oil
Company, $40.

1927 Official Road Map of Arizona, California, Washington, Oregon, British Columbia
Union Oil Company, $15.

1936 Texas Centennial Exposition Map, Texas
and Oklahoma,
The Texas Company, $15.

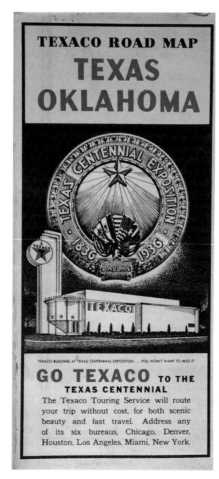

1929 Road Map of Montana, Continental Oil
Company, $40.

1931 Road Map, Nebraska, Deep-Rock Prize Oils, $30.

In Delaware-Maryland, Virginia-W. Virginia, Richfield Oil Corp. of New York, $25.

How to Get More Miles from Your Tires, Allstate Tires, Sears Roebuck and Co., $15.

Cascade International Highway, $15.

Texaco Road Map Kansas, Nebraska, $25.

Texaco Road Ma[p]
Ohio, $25.

Tour Oklahoma with Texaco, no pricing.

Tour Oklahoma with Texaco.

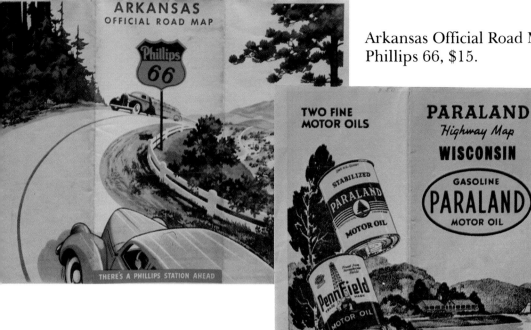

Arkansas Official Road Map, 1931,
Phillips 66, $15.

1948 Highway Map,
Wisconsin, Paraland
Motor Oil, $30.

1935 North Dakota, South Dakota, Pure Oil
Pathfinder,
Pure Oil Company, $10.

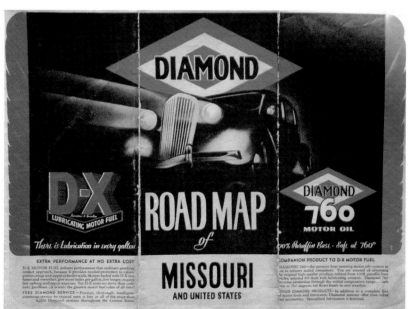

Diamond Road Map of Missouri, $10.

1931 Travel Illinois, the Land of Pleasure,
Conoco Travel Bureau, $10.

Motoring Map, W. Virginia, Virginia, Mary
land, and Delaware, Keystone Gasoline, $1

1940 Iowa Official Road Map, Phillips 66,
$10.

1936 Highway Map, North & South Dakota,
Phillips Petroleum Company, $15.

1933 Road Map, Chicago and Vicinity, Sinclair, $40.

Indiana Road Map, Sinclair, $30.

Arkansas, Louisiana, Mississippi Road Map, (believe to be 1935) Sinclair, $30.

Florida Road Map, (believe to be 1936) Sinclair, $30.

Illinois Road Map, Sinclair, $30.

Illinois Road Map, Sinclair, $30.

1934 Oklahoma Road Map, Sinclair, $25

1924 Auto Trails in New England, Socony
Gasoline & Motor Oil, $15.

1928 New England in Soconyland, Socony Gasoline & Motor Oil, $15.

1925 Road Map of New England, Socony Gasoline & Motor Oil, $15.

1929 New England in Soconyland, Socony Gasoline & Motor Oil, $15.

1930 New York in Soconyland, Socony Gasoline & Motor Oil, $15.

Tydol Trails thru Massachusetts, Tide Water
Oil Company, $10.

1934 Richfield "Strip Maps", California,
Oregon, Washington, $10.

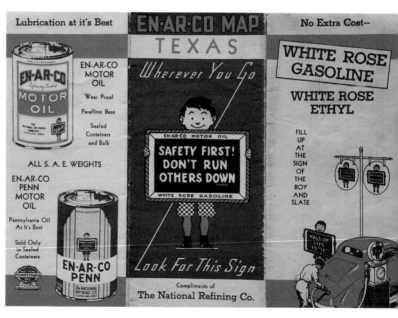

1931 EN-AR-CO Map, Texas, The National
Refining Company, $20.

1931 Arkansas Road Map, Marathon Oil
Company, $25.

1941 Massachusetts, Connecticut, Rhode Island, Tide Water Associated Oil Company, $10.

1935 Massachusetts, Connecticut, Rhode Island, Richfield, $15.

1929 New England, Beacon Colonial Products, $20.

1927 Tydol Trails thru' New England, $10.

Atlantic Road Map Pennsylvania, Delaware,
New Jersey, Washington, D.C., (possible teens)
Atlantic Refining Company, $10.

1926 Auto Trails Map,
Harris Oils, $10.

1934, Nebraska Road Map, Standard Oil
Company, $15.

1936 Texas Road Map, Standard Oil Company, $15.

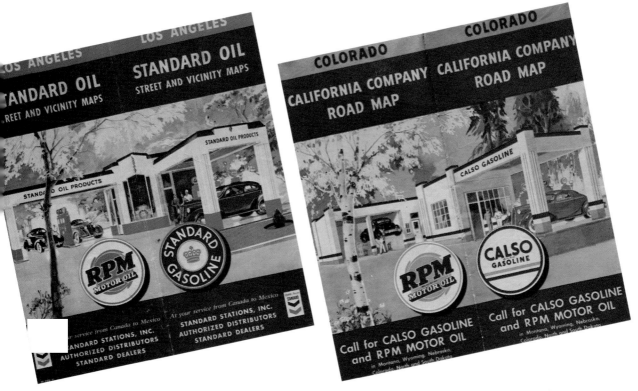

Los Angeles Street and Vicinity Maps, Standard Oil Company, $15.

1939 Colorado Road Map, Calso Gasoline and Motor Oil, $15.

Supreme Motor Oil, $10.

1924 Lower New England, Gulf Refining Company, $10.

Ontario and Quebec Info-Map Gulf Refining Company, $15.

1916 New England, Gulf Refining Company, $10.

Record of Lubrication, Tires, and Gasoline (possibly teens), Gulf Refining Company, $15.

1927 California, Nevada, Gulf Refining Company, $20.

1929 Delaware, Maryland, Virginia, West Virginia Automobile Road Map, Gulf Refining Company, $20.

Chapter Three

Motorcans

The following is a very good example of how
oil companies utilized motor-driven art to
advertise their products.

Stabl-Flo, $10.

Racing Sta-Lube, StaLube, Inc., $45.

Motor Graphite, K. W. Graphite
Corp., $35.

Ronson, $100.

Penntroleum Motor Oil, Cato Oil
and Grease Company, $65.

Century Limited Motor Oil,
Century Oil Products Co., $75.

Hudson Motor Oil,
Hudson Oil Co., $85.

Aero Motor Oil, Allied Oil Co., $75.

Phoenix (3 photos, 3 sides), Phoenix Oil Co.,
Inc., $150.

Triple "L" Long Life Lube, $75.

Top Flite Motor Oil $80.

New Texaco Airplane Oil, The Texas Company and Golden West Motor Oil, Golden West Oil Company, pricing unknown.

Duplex Marine Engine Oil, Quaker State Oil Refining Corp., $75.

Fleetwood Aero Craft Motor Oil, Traymore Lubricants, $95.

StratosOil "New" Premium Type, $75.

Fleet H-D Motor Oil, Elreco
Motor Oil, $80.

Tulane Motor Oil, $90.

Ace Wil-Flo Motor Oil, $65.

Texaco Marine Motor Oil, The Texas Company, $75.

Speed-way Motor Oil, Speedway Petroleum
Corp., $65.

Whiz 30 Below Zero Motor Oil, $45.

D-A Speed-Sport Oil, D-A Lubricant Company, Inc., $35.

Hudson Premium, Hudson Oil Co., $85.

Elf Presti "s"
20W 50, $75

ZeroPruf AntiFreeze, $45.

Racing StaLube Motor Oil, StaLube, Inc., $45.

Fleetwood Aero Craft Motor Oil, $45.

Signal Outboard Motor
Oil, $30.

Withrows Premium Motor Oil, $35.

Atlantic Motor Oil, Aviation, The Atlantic
Refining Company, $45.

Cen-Pe-Co Super Racing Oil, $45.

Chapter Four

Pin-backs, Name Badges, Signs, Globes

As you will see, assembled here is an excellent sampling of pin-backs, name badges, signs, and globes.

Small Mobil Ashtray, Mobil Oil Company, $90.

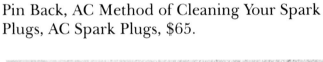

Texaco Window Decal, The Texas Company, $40.

Pin Back, AC Method of Cleaning Your Spark Plugs, AC Spark Plugs, $65.

Texaco Marfak No. 0, The Texas Company, $55.

Texaco Motor Cup Grease Can, The Texas
Company, $55.

Caltex Extra Heavy Duty Motor
Oil, Texaco, $50.

Caltex Extra Heavy Duty Motor Oil,
(1 quart can), Texaco, $55.

Caltex Extra Heavy Duty Motor Oil,
(1 gallon can), Texaco, $50.

En-Ar-Co Motor Oil Bank, Canadian Oil
Companies Limited, $150.

Sunoco Oil Ink Blotter, Sun Oil, $25.

Sunoco 'Nu-Blue' Ink Blotter, Sun Oil, $25.

Texaco Ink Blotter, Texaco, $40.

Texaco Ink Blotter, Texaco, $40.

Texaco Motor Oil Ink Blotter, Texaco, $40.

Texaco Fire Chief Shirt, Texaco, pricing un
known.

Texhoma Gasoline Coin Tray, $40.

Route 66 Motor Oil, (two gallon can), $65.

Motor Graphite Upper Cylinder Lubricant, K-W Graphite Corp., $45.

Whiz Service Center, $200.

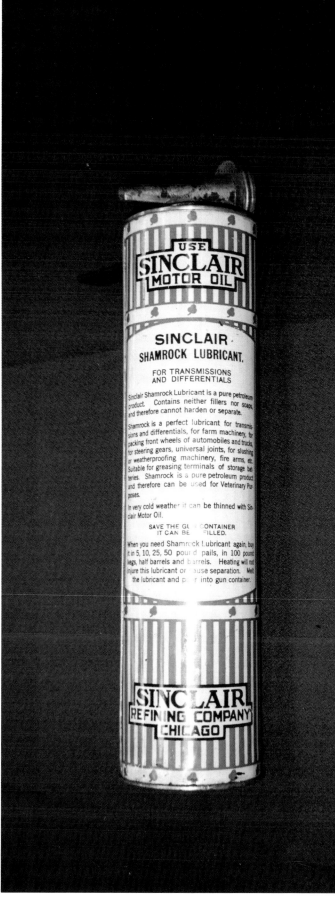

Sinclair Shamrock Lubricant, Sinclair Refining Co., Chicago, pricing unknown.

Sinclair Shamrock Lubricant, Sinclair Refining Co., Chicago.

Champion Spark Plugs Clock, $275.

Santa Claus Mail Box, Gulf Oil & Refining, pricing unknown.

Linco Gasoline Oils Pin Back, $35.

Honorary Pilot Flying 'A' Gasoline, Pin Back Tydol, $35.

Road Supreme Gasoline Globe, pricing unknown.

Champlin Oils Pin Back, Oil Change Reminder, Champlin, $30.

Vote For Husky Pin Back, Husky, $30.

Sun Light Oil Watch Fob, Kansas City Oil, $85.

Capitol Automobile Oil Wa[tch] Fob, The Uncle Sam Oil Company, $75.

Dixie Pump Plate, McNutt Oil & Refining Co., Inc., $250.

Atlantic White Flash Pin Back,
Atlantic Gas and Oil, $25.

Gulf's Comic Weekly Pin Back, Gulf Oil and
Refining, $25.

Socony Gasoline Pin Back, Standard Oil
Company of N.Y., $30.

High Grade Lubricating Oils Pin Back, Zone
Oil Company, $75.

Silver Anniversary Phillips 66 Pin Back,
Phillips Petroleum Company, $25.

Koolmotor Bronze Gasolene Pin Back, Cities Service, $20.

Hi-Speed Attendant's Name Badge, Hi-Speed, pricing unknown.

Lubricating & Illuminating Oils Pin Back, Union Petroleum Company, Philadelphia, Stewart Union Oil Co., St. Louis, $35.

Socony Attendant's Name Badge, Standard Oil Company of N.Y., pricing unknown.

From Coast to Coast Independent Oil Pin Back, Quincy Gasoline, $35.

Esso Hat Badge, Esso, pricing unknown.

Texaco Attaché Case, The Texas Company, pricing unknown.

Republic Pump Plate, Royale, $125.

Jenny Pump Gage, (early) Jenny Manufacturing, pricing unknown.

En-Ar-Co Separator Oil, Canadian Oil Companies Ltd., $90.

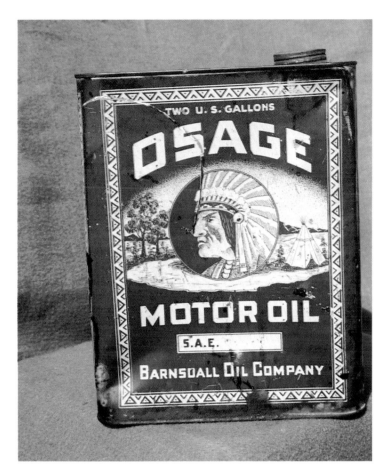

OSAGE Motor Oil, (2 U.S. Gallons), Barnsdall Oil Company, $120.

Phillips 66 Motor Oil, (1 Gallon), Phillips Petroleum Company, $90.

Champlin Motor Oil, (1/2 Gallon), Champlin Refining Company, $75.

Korco Auto Oil, (1/2 Gallon), Kansas Oil
Refining Co., $70.

Rear

Front

Power-Lube Motor Oil, (5 quarts) (top part of
can is missing),
Power-Lube, pricing unknown.

Cattle - Horses and other Livestock, (1 Gallon), Phillips Petroleum Company, $90.

TP Thurman Grease, Texas Pacific Coal And Oil Company, $40.

Cosden Liquid Gas, Cosden Oils, $80 for three piece glass globe.

Champlin Motor Oil, (1/2 gallon), Champlin Refining Co., $65.

Gilmore Lubricant, Gilmore, $90.

Panhandle Globe, (15" metal-band globe),
Panhandle Gasoline, $350.

Texaco Air Pump, The Texas Company, $350.

Pennzoil Outboard Motor Oil, (glass container, paper label), Pennzoil, $50.

Hudson Motor Oil, (glass container, paper label), Hudson Oil Company, $50.

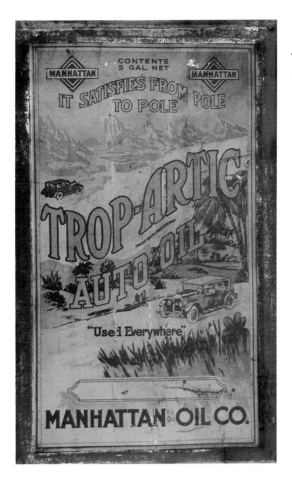

Trop-Artic Auto Oil, (5 gallon), Manhattan Oil Company, pricing unknown.

Marco-Penn World's Premium Oil, (2 gallons), Martin Oil Company, $65.

Sunoco Price Sign, Sun Oil Company, $225.

Mobiloil Arctic 20-20W, Mobil Oil, pricing unknown.

Mobiloil Arctic, Mobil Oil, pricing unknown.

Mobiloil "AF", Mobil Oil, pricing unknown.

Mobiloil Arctic Special 10W, Mobil Oil, pricing
unknown.

Mobiloil "BB", Mobil Oil, pricing unknown.

Martin's Super Regular, Martin Oil Company, $275.

Martin's Premium Ethyl, Martin Oil Company, $26

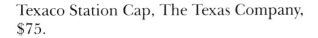

Cloverleaf Globe, (plastic body), $140.

Texaco Station Cap, The Texas Company, $75.

Aeroshell Oil, (note Nazi insignia on cup grease can), pricing unknown.

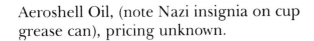

Havoline Oil Banner, Indian Refining, $75.

World's Lowest Prices pricing book, 1932, The Pep Boys, $40.

Pullman Anti-Freeze, $45.

Sunoco Battery Power Meter, Sun Oil Company, $65.

Power King Premium, Power King Ethyl, (three-piece glass), pricing unknown.

Gas Motor Velv-O-Lene Oils, (15" metal-band globe), Cleburne Oil Company, $275.

Red Hat Motor Oil & Gasoline, (15" metal-band globe), $550.

Dependable Lubrication for your Motor, (1/2 gallon), $95.

Once-Always, (1/2 gallon), Cities Service Oil
Company, $45.

Pennfield Motor Oil, (1/2 gallon), The Quaker
Petroleum Company, Inc., $65.

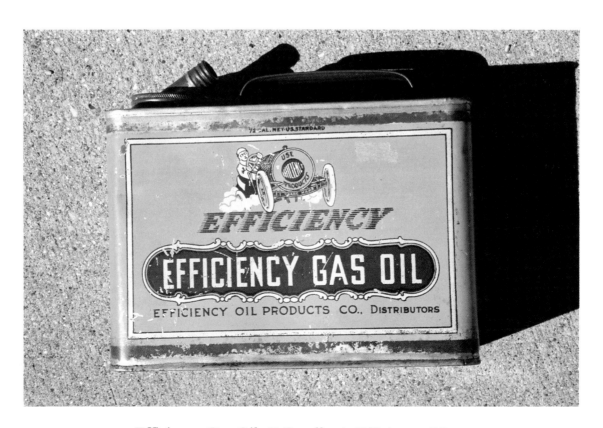

Efficiency Gas Oil, (1/2 gallon), Efficiency Oil
Products Co., $125.

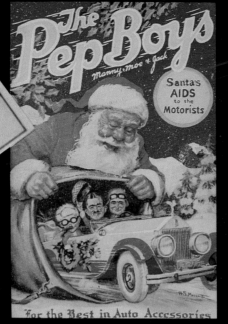

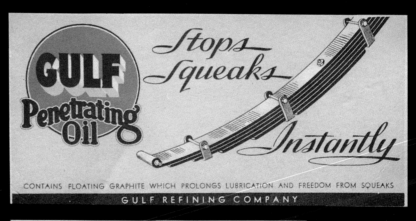

Texaco Motor Oil Ink Blotter, The Texas Company, $35.

Santa's Aids to the Motorist Magazine, The Pep Boys, $

Stops Squeaks Instantly Ink Blotter, Gulf Refining, $25.

Mobiloil Arctic Ink Blotter, Standard Oil Company of N.Y., $25.

Socony Cold Test Motor Oil Ink Blot Standard Oil Company of N.Y., $25

Socony Motor Oil Ink Blotter, Standard Oil
Company of N.Y., $40.

What the New and Better Texaco Gasoline
Will Do For You, (advertising piece from
Texaco), $65.

Texaco Tire Service, (tire inspection history
from Texaco), The Texas Company, $75.

A Half Charged Battery, (battery inspection
history from Texaco), The Texas Company,
$60.

What Every Tourist needs, (two-sided Easy
Pour advertising piece from Texaco), The
Texas Company, $60.

The Texaco Easy Pour Can.

Texaco Fire-Chief Gasoline, Texaco Crack-Proof Motor Oil,
(two-sided advertising piece from Texaco),
The Texas Company, $60.

There's No Better Combination For Winter Driving.

Hood Tires, (4" die-cut advertising piece),
$120.

Aviation Products Station Cap, Pure Oil, $120.

Qckwork Metal Polish, The Texas Company,
$450.

Texaco Motor Oil, Heavy, The Texas Company, $65.

Sinclair Stock Spray, (1 gallon), Sinclair Refining, $45.

Miscellaneous display of 5 cans, Various Companies, pricing unknown.

Texaco Alarm Clock, The Texas Company,
$275.

Caltex Glass for Gasoline Pump, (5" advertising plate), The Texas Company, $55.

Smith-O-Lene Aviation Gasoline, (large, cut
for neon), Smith-O-Lene Company, pricing
unknown.

Gilmore Miniature Pump, (handmade advertising piece), Gilmore, pricing unknown.

Be Square Motor Oil, (30" curb sign),
Barnsdall, $175.

Texaco Attendant Name Badges, The Texas
Company, $175.

Texaco Diesel Fuel Globe, (plastic body globe),
The Texas Company, $220.

Texaco Petroleum Products, (1 gallon), The
Texas Company, $70.

Texaco Radiator Cleaner, The Texas Company, $50.

Havoline Automobile Cylinder Oil, Havoline Oil Company, Indian Refining, $75.

Texaco Spica Oil, (1 pint), The Texas Company, $55.

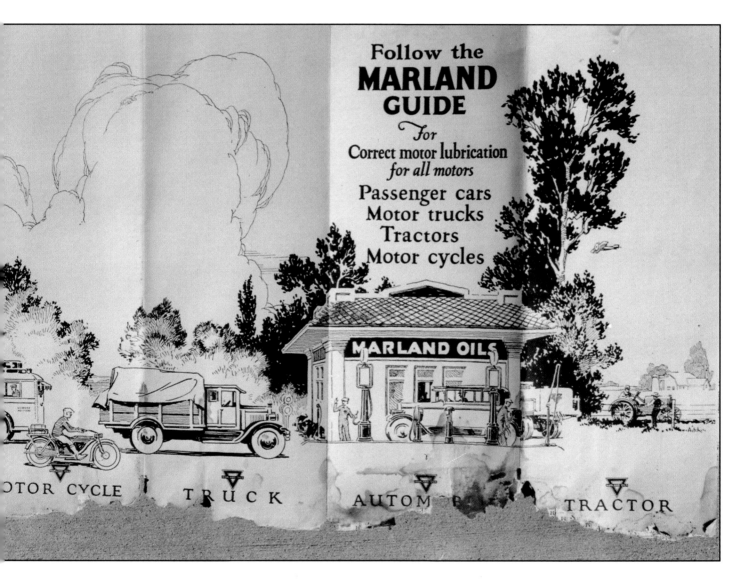

Follow the Marland Guide, (correct motor lubrication for all motors), Marland Oil Company, pricing unknown.

Conoco Motor Oil, (two-sided sign),
Conoco, pricing unknown.

Wadhams Tempered Motor Oil, Wadhams Oil,
pricing unknown.

Mother Penn Motor Oil, (two-sided small
lubster sign), Dryer Clark & Dryer Oil Company, $140.

Globe Gasoline,
(30" sign), $425.

Chapter Five

Signs

This section contains everything from the small pump-plate signs to the larger marquee signs that were displayed to attract customers.

Keystone POWERFUEL, Keystone Gasoline Company, (pump plate sign), $225.

Cresyl Regular 'Knock Free', Cresyl Gasoline, (small pump plate sign), $175.

AMLICO Premium Gasoline, AMLICO Gasoline, (small pump plate sign), $200.

Solvenized JENNEY, Hy-Power, Jenney Manufacturing Company, (small pump plate), pricing unknown.

CALSO Supreme Gasoline, (small pump plate), California Standard, $175.

Mobilgas SPECIAL Gasoline, Mobil Oil Company, (small pump plate), $150.

Texaco 'Marine White' Gasoline, Texaco Oil
Company, (small pump plate), $400.

Texaco Outboard Blend, Texaco Oil Company, $175.

'Be Square To Your Motor Barnsdall (very small lubster sign), $100.

Gilmore Lion Head Motor Oil, Monarch of Oil, Gilmore Gas and Oil, (the sign that is pictured may be reproduction), $200.

Certified Water ATLAS Battery Service, Atlas Battery, $90.

Texaco Motor Oil, Texaco, (Unusual & rare sign from Australia), $350.

Cities Service, Cities Service Gasoline, (42" sign), $175.

Caltex Havoline 'Bespaart U geld!', Caltex by Texaco from Germany, $300.

Fina Agent Sign, Fina Gasoline, $250.

Sinclair Gasoline, Sinclair Gas & Oil, $60.

Good Rich Tire and
Battery, $75.

Large LION Gasoline Sign, Lion Gas & Oil,
(42" sign), $190.

'Help Keep This Place Clean', Sunray Oils,
$175.

Derby Motor Oil, Derby Oil Company, (42"
sign), $140.

Texaco Ethyl, Ethyl Gasoline Corporation, (30" curb sign), $475.

Humble Gasoline, Humble Oil & Gas, (42" sign), $340.

Good Year TIRES! TIRES! TIRES!, (The Sinclaire Dino is advertising with Good Year), (small tin sign), $55.

Gargoyle Mobiloil Mobilgas, Mobil Oil, (large early sign), $370.

Texas Pacific Ethyl Gasoline, Texas Pacific Oil
& Gas, (30" sign), $290.

Marathon Ethyl, Marathon Gasoline, (30"
sign), $275.

Flying A Motor Diesel, (large sign), $225.

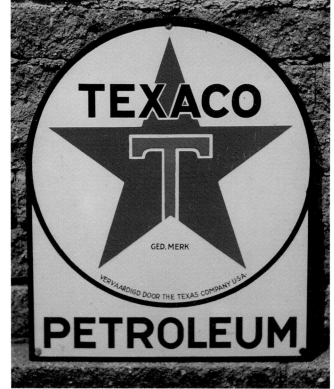

Texaco Petroleum, Texaco (European Sign), (small lubster sign), $275.

Skylark Gasoline, (small pump plate), pricing unknown.

SAVMOR PL Gasoline, (small pump plate), $325.

Sinclair Aircraft, Sinclair Gas & Oil, (42" sign), pricing unknown.

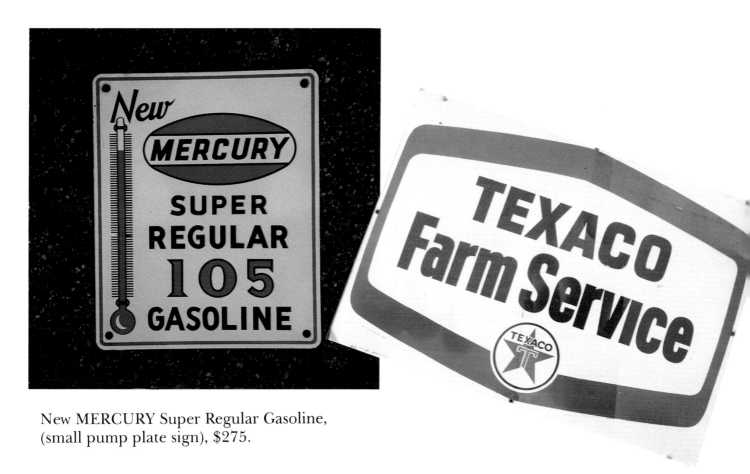

New MERCURY Super Regular Gasoline,
(small pump plate sign), $275.

Texaco Farm Service, Texaco Company, $175.

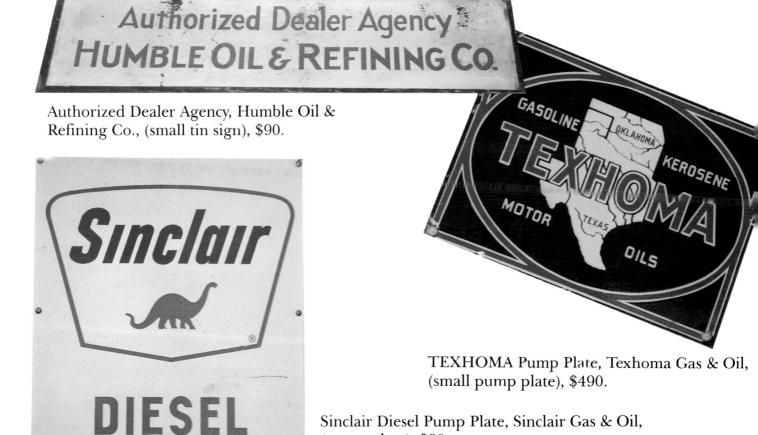

Authorized Dealer Agency, Humble Oil &
Refining Co., (small tin sign), $90.

TEXHOMA Pump Plate, Texhoma Gas & Oil,
(small pump plate), $490.

Sinclair Diesel Pump Plate, Sinclair Gas & Oil,
(pump plate), $90.

Texaco Motor Oil Lubster Sign, Texaco Company, $175.

Amalie Motor Oil, $90.

Stays FULL Longer (tin sign), Texaco Company, $300.

Mobil (Large two-sided sign), Mobil Oil Company, $125.

Texas Pacific, (large), TP Gasoline and Motor
Oil, (42" sign), $375.

Standard NO SMOKING, Standard Oil Company, $150.

Humble (small truck-door sign), Humble Oil
& Refining, $140.

United Service Motors, (large two-sided sign),
$600.

Texaco Aviation Fuels & Lubricants, (painted metal sign), Texaco Company, $375.

Flying A Gas, (large double-sided sign), $400.

Greyhound Motor Fuel, Greyhound Oil Company, $325.

Royaline Gasoline, Royaline Oil Company, $175.

Magnolia Gasoline (unusual), Socony Motor Oil Company, $375.

ACE HIGH Gas-Oil, pricing unknown.

Shellubrication 'The Modern Upkeep Service', Shell Oil Company, $350.

Frontier Rarin' To - Go. Large two sided. The Frontier Refining Company, $450.

Stanocola Petroleum Products, Standard Oil Co. of Louisiana, $400.

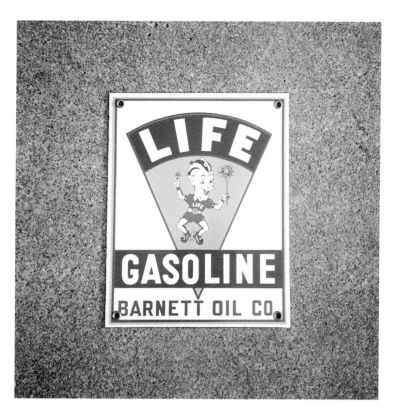

Life Gasoline, Barnett Oil Co., (small pump plate), pricing unknown.

D-X Sunray, (small one-sided), $250.

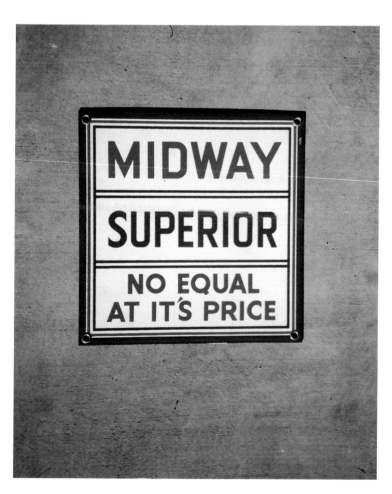

Midway Superior, (pump plate), $100.

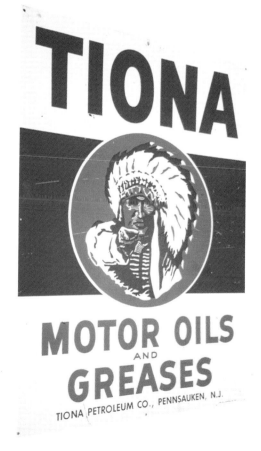

Tiona Motor Oils & Greases (tin), Tiona Petroleum Company, $150.

Fleet Motor Oil - Grease, The K-T Oil Corporation, (small tin sign), $160.

2 Qts. Texaco Easy Pour Can, (small rare
sign), pricing unknown.

Globe Gasoline, (30" sign), $225.

VARCON Motor Oil, (die-cut cardboard),
$225.

Kendall's Dynamic New Gas, (die-cut cardboard), pricing unknown.

Mobiloil Arctic, (die-cut cardboard), Mobil Oil
Company, $250.

Wm. Penn Motor Oil, $175.

Continental (flanged tire sign), $125.

Invader Motor Oil, (embossed painted tin),
$325.

Mohawk ('Time-to-Return' sign), Mohawk Tire Company, $60.

Red Indian Motor Oil, $135.

Shell Gasoline, (die-cut sign), Shell Oil Company, $390.

Polarine Motor Oil, (early 30" sign), Standard Gasoline, $240.

Johnson '70' Gasolene, (die-cut tin), $350.

Essence Girtex (flanged sign), Texaco Company, $390.

Veedol Motor Oil, (cardboard sign), pricing unknown.

Marine Gasoline, (large die-cut sign), $550.

Pennant Oils (small sign), Pierce Oil Corporation, $340.

Sweney Sky Hawk Gasoline, (painted tin sign), $300.

Hancock Gasoline pump plate, $450.

Diamond Tires, (painted flanged sign), $1

Shell Gasoline, (small rare sign), Shell Oil Company, $480.

Red Crown Gasoline, Standard Oil Company, $450.

Gasco Motor Fuel, $475.

Phillips 66 Motor Oil,
(30" sign), $360.

Use CHAMPLIN Oils, Champlin Oil Company, $180.

Standard Red Crown pump plate, Standard Oil Company, (small pump plate), $85.

Mobilgas, Mobil Oil Company, $300.

eLreco Gasoline, (30" sign), $340.

Wilcox Ethyl Gasoline, (30" sign), $190.

Waverly Ethyl Gasoline, $190.

Red Chief Ethyl Gasoline, (30" sign), $190.

'Be Square to Your Motor', Barnsdall, pricing unknown.

Fill Up With ARTIC-WATER, (small cardboard), $70.

Shamrock No. 1 Diesel, (small pump plate sign), $75.

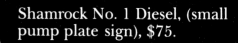

Mobilgas, (30" sign), $175.

Chevron Supreme Gasoline, (small cardboard), $75.

Brilliant bronze, Johnson Oil Company, (small pump plate), $150.

Gargoyle Mobiloil, Mobil Oil Company, $200.

Crown Gasoline, Standard Oil Company, (flanged sign), $250.

Sunray Safety Sign, Sunray Oil Company,
$175.

Vickers Gasoline Friendly Service, Vickers
Petroleum Products, (approx. 8' X 4.5'), $350.

Mobil Pipe Line Sign, Socony-Vacuum, $100.

Texaco Pipe Line Sign, Texaco Company,
$100.

Socony Safety First, Standard Oil Co. of N.Y.,
$125.

Skytane Ethyl, (small pump plate), $190.

Sampson Gasoline, Mutual Oil Company,
(embossed tin sign), $80.

Veedol Service Ahead,
(large tin sign), $190.

Johnson 'Time Tells', Johnson Motor Oil, (42"
sign), $475.

Waggoner Refining Co., Inc., Waggoner
Petroleum Products, (42" rare sign), $475.

Sinclair Gasoline, (cardboard), $90.

Keynoil Lubricates & Lasts, White Eagle
Motor Oil, (small sign), $225.

Texaco Industrial Lubricants, (small embossed
tin), $75.

Jenney Super-Aero, Jenney Manufacturing
Company, $250.

Texaco Marine Lubricants, Texaco Company, $275.

Humble Clean Rest Room sign, Humble Refining, $140.

Mobil Clean Rest Room sign, Mobil Oil Company, $175.

Sanitary Rest Room, $75.

We Sell Socony Motor Gasoline, Standard Oil Company of N.Y., $250.

TP round sign with edge, (may be either RR or gasoline sign), pricing unknown.

Rest Rooms sign, (Conoco), $190.

Pride of Oregon, (large pump plate sign), $450.

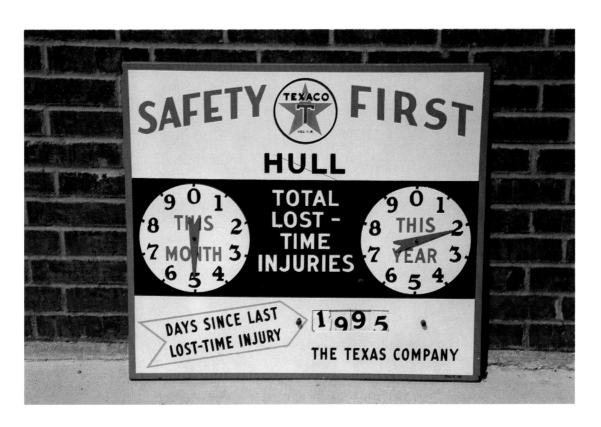

Texaco Safety First sign, The Texas Company,
$1100.

Humble Aviation Products, Humble Petroleum
Products, (very large sign), pricing unknown.

Texaco Marine White, Texaco Company, $160.

Cadillac Service sign
(42" early sign), pric
unknown.

Crystalite, The Texas Company, U.S.A.,
(flanged foreign sign) pricing unknown.

Bear Wheel & Steering, (small one-sided
painted sign), $190.

Chapter Six

Pictorial Cans

Most, if not all, pictorial cans displayed here are some of the most graphic and colorful quart cans available.

Cosden, Premium Type, Cosden Oil Company, $110.

Marathon, Best in the Long Run (4 cans),
Marathon Oil Company, pricing unknown.

Indian Motor Cycle (2 cans), Indian
Motocycle Company, pricing unknown.

Master Outboard, More Speed More Power,
$150.

Oneida Motor Oil, West Penn
Oil Company, $120.

Pure As Gold Motor Oil, The Pep Boys,
Manny, Moe and Jack, $110.

Big Chief Heavy Duty Motor Oil, Mid-West
Oil Company, $110.

Red Giant Oil, Red Giant
Oil Company, $35.

Oilzum Motor Oil and Lubricants, The White
& Bagley Company, $140.

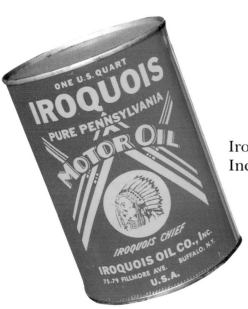

Iroquois Motor Oil, Iroquois Oil Company,
Inc., $40.

Silent Chief Motor Oil, $260.

Tiopet Racing Oil, Tiona
Petroleum Company, $275.

LaHuronne, Huile A Moteur,
Canada Specialitees Limitee,
Quebec, $35.

Penn-Rolene, The King of Motor Oil, William Roth and Sons Oil Company, $60.

PennThrift, Radbill Oil Company, $40.

Admiral Penn, Pennsylvania Oil, H.K. Stahl Company, $30.

Oilzum Motor Oils and Lubricants, The White & Bagley Company, $145.

Eskimo AntiFreeze, Thompson, $40.

Eskimo AntiFreeze, Monsanto, $35.

Concho Perfect Lubrication, United Oil & Grease Company, $90.

Stop & Go, Union Petroleum
Company, $170.

Iroquois Motor Oil, Iroquios Oil Company,
pricing unknown.

Blue Bonnet Economical
Motor Oil, $70.

Tan-Kar Motor Oil, Tan-Kar
Oil Co., $75.

J-D-D Motor Oil, J-D-D Lubricants Company,
$30.

Rotary Motor, $25.

Midland Motor Oil, $45.

Harley-Davidson Motor Cycles Oil, Harley-Davidson Motor Company, pricing unknown.

Aeroil, Cleans as it Lubricates, Universal Oil Company of Texas, pricing unknown.

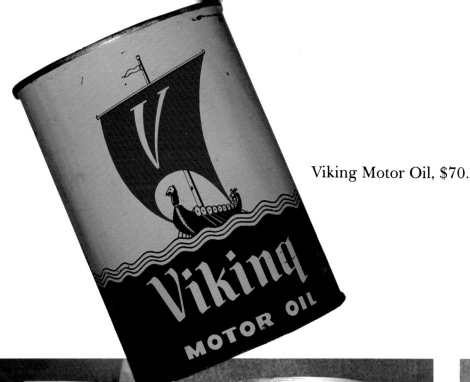

Viking Motor Oil, $70.

Golden West Motor Oil, Golden West Petroleum Company, Inc., pricing unknown.

Phillips 66, The World's Finest OIL for your MOTOR, $45.

Shell Penn, $80.

Dutch Mill, 100% Pure Pennyslvania Motor Oil, $65.

Gebharts Gold Comet Motor Oil, $30.

Terrys Penn-Oil Motor Oil, Terry Carpenter, $40.

Gold Star Motor Oil, The Star Oil Company, $45.

Blue Pennant, Maritime Oil Company, $30.

Ray Lube Motor Oil, Molaco
Oil Company, $30.

Hi-Tex Motor Oil, Airline Oil & Grease Company, $80.

Comet Motor Oil, $60.

Premium Rock Penn Motor Oil, $50.

Packard Special Motor Oil, Tested and
Studebaker Packard Approved, $25.

Inter-State XL-Penn Motor Oil, Inter-State
Oil Company, $20.

PennField Motor Oil, Pennfield Oil Company,
$25.

Bellube Motor Oil, The Bell Oil and Gas
Company, $40.

Climatic, Good the World Over, Gentry Oil &
Grease Company, Inc., $30.

Snowman Flotex Anti-Freeze, Windsor-Lloyd
Products, Inc., $45.

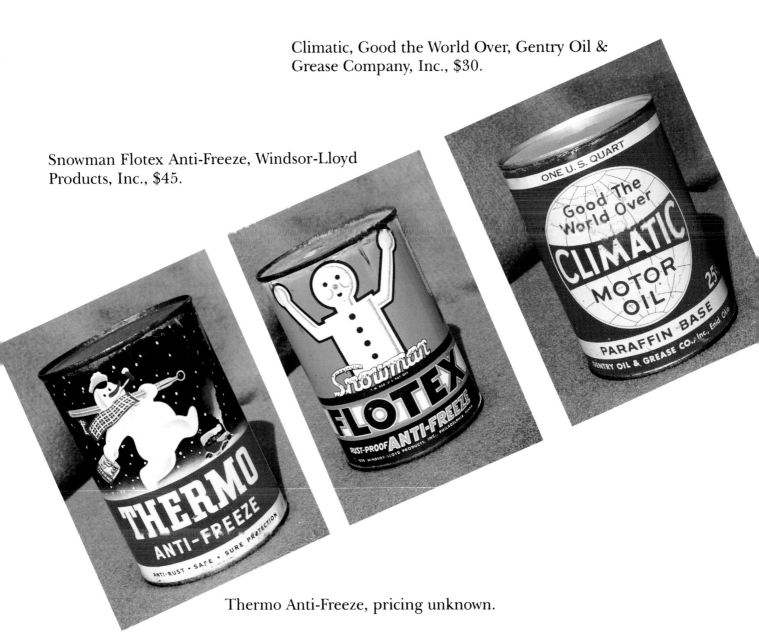

Thermo Anti-Freeze, pricing unknown.

Northland Penn Motor Oil, Northland Oil
Company, Roosevelt Oil Company, $20.

Autoline Oil XP triple protection, America's
Oldest Oil Company, $20.

Jenney Solvenoil Motor Oil, Jenney Paraffine
Base Auto Oil, Jenney Auto Oil, $20.

U - S Certified Motor Oil, U.S. Oil Company, $20.

Lou-Bob Motor Oil, Lou-Bob Company, $20.

Wm. Penn Motor Oils, Wm. Penn Motor Oil, Canfield Oil Company, $45.

Mother Penn Motor Oil, Dryer Clark & Dryer Oil Company, pricing unknown.

Falcon Motor Oil, $120.

Pioneer Motor Oil, $270.

Thorobred Speed Stamina, Blue Ribbon Oil
Co., $260.

Pioneer Motor Oil, $200.

Frontier Rarin'
To Go, $70.

Powerlube Motor Oil, Smooth as the Thread of a Tiger, $450.

Husky Motor Oil, Western Oil & Fuel Co., $250.

Mobiloil Aero Green Band, $110.

Husky Motor Oil, Western Oil & Fuel Co., $250.

Jayhawk Oils, $110.

Sovereign Dual Mileage
Motor Oil, $45.

SeaGull Motor Oil, $80.

Hancock Premium Motor
Oil, $40.

Monarch Petroleum Products,
pricing unknown.

Sinclair Motor Oil, Mellowed 100 Million
Years, pricing unknown.

Vacuum processed Motor Oil, Products that Speak for Themselves, Pennsylvania Oil Terminal, Inc., $100.

En-Ar-Co Penn, The National Refining Company, $45.

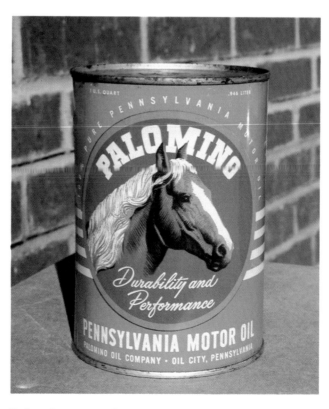

Palomino Durability and Performance, Pennsylvania Motor Oil, $550.

Owens Pendragon Motor Oil, Owens-Illinois
Oil Company, $90.

Columbia Motor Oil, $75.

Super Frigidtest
Anti-Freeze, $40.

Richlube Premium Motor Oil, $40.

Magnolia Lubrite Motor Oil, Socony-Vacuum
Oil Company, $55.

Husky Multi-Viscosity Motor Oil, Western Oil
& Fuel Company, $90.

Mobiloil Aero White Band, Socony-Vacuum
Oil Company, $110.

Mobiloil Aero Red Band, Socony-Vacuum Oil
Company, $110.

Chapter Seven
Soda Signs

Nichol Kola, Twice as Good, $90.

Grape Ola, It's REAL Grape, $75.

A Bunch of Grapes from
Welch Juniors, $90.

Coca-Cola, $100.

Dr. Pepper, Good for Life, (flanged sign),
Bottle: 10 2 4, $250.

Dr. Pepper, Good for Life, $35.

Dr. Pepper, Good for Life, (flanged sign),
Clock indicates: 10 2 4, $150.

Dr. Pepper, Good for Life, Clock indicates: 10
2 4, $250.

Dr. Pepper, Good for Life, (door Push), Two
clocks indicate: 10 2 4, $400.

Ice Cold Coca-Cola (gas pricing sign), $150.

Barq's "It's Good" Ice Cold, (gas pricing sign), $150.

Drink MOXIE Distinctively Different, $400.

Dr. Pepper, Good for Life, $125.

NuGrape, A Flavor You Cant Forget, (flanged sign), $75.

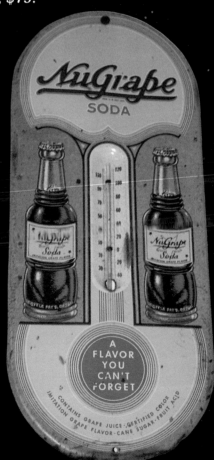

NuGrape Soda (thermometer), $160.

Thank You, Call Again - Dr. Pepper, $150.

MORE SERVICE STATIONS FROM...

Filling Station Collectibles Rick Pease. Some of the hottest collectibles today reflect our passions for the automobile. This book pictures filling station memorabilia, motoring products, and automotive advertisements in vivid color. From the turn of the century to modern times, the hundreds of filling station collectibles on display in this book fill 563 color photographs and an up-to-date price guide.

Size: 8 1/2" x 11" Price Guide 144 pp.
563 color photos
ISBN: 0-88740-643-2 soft cover $29.95

Gas Station Collectibles Sonya Stenzler and Rick Pease. Nearly 1000 color photographs of the nostalgic and often beautiful artifacts show some of the best of the collectibles available to the eager collectors of items from service stations.

Size: 8 1/2" x 11" Price guide 160 pp.
Nearly 1000 color photos
ISBN: 0-88740-496-0 soft cover $29.95

SCHIFFER PUBLISHING

77 Lower Valley Road. Atglen, PA 19310
(610) 593-1777